Stars and Planets

Carole Stott

KINGFISHER

First published 2011 by Kingfisher
an imprint of Macmillan Children's Books
a division of Macmillan Publishers Limited
20 New Wharf Road, London N1 9RR
Basingstoke and Oxford
Associated companies throughout the world
www.panmacmillan.com

Illustrations by: Peter Bull Art Studio

ISBN 978-0-7534-3034-7

1 3 5 7 9 8 6 4 2
1TR/1210/WKT/UNTD/140MA

A CIP catalogue record for this book is available from
the British Library.

Printed in China

FOR RUBY, MARTHA AND ELIZA

Picture credits

**The Publisher would like to thank the following
for permission to reproduce their material.
(t = top, b = bottom, c = centre, l = left, r = right):**
Pages 4tl & 4cr Hubble/NASA/STSci; 4bl Shutterstock/Plutonius
3d; 5cl NASA/University of Arizona; 5br Photolibrary/The Travel
Library; 6tl Science Photo Library (SPL)/Jerry Schad; 8cl SPL/G
Bacon/European Space Agency (ESA)/NASA/STSci; 8bl SPL/
Larry Landolfi; 8br Hubble/NASA/STSci; 9tl & 9tr Hubble/NASA/
STSci; 9b European Space Observatory; 10bl NASA; 12l & 12br
NASA/Apollo Program; 12cr Photolibary/Comstock; 13t & 13bl
NASA/Apollo Program; 13r SPL/Eckhard Slawik; 14tl European
Space Observatory; 16l NASA/Hinode; 16tc NASA/German
Aerospace Center/DLR; 16br ESO/Philippe Federici; 17tr NASA/
Hubble; 17cl NASA/US Geological Survey; 17bl SPL/Mark
Garlick; 17br SPL/Mark Garlick; 18bl NASA/JPL; 20bl SPL/
Francis Menage/Starsem; 20cr SPL/NASA; 21t SPL/NASA;
21bl SPL/Ria Novosti; 21tr & 21br ESA; 22b SPL/Detlev van
Ravenswaay; 24l, 24r & 25t ISS/NASA; 25tr, 25cl & 25cr SPL/
NASA; 25bl & 25br NASA; 26tl ESA; 28cl NASA/JPL; 28bl
NASA/Cornell University; 28tr SPL/David Ducros; 29cl NASA/
JPL; 29tr ESA; 29bc NASA/Goddard Space Flight Center; 29br
NASA/JPL; 30tl SPL/Tony & Daphne Hallas; 30cl Photolibrary/
Peter Arnold; 30cr & 30br ESA; 31tr, 31c, 31bc ISS/NASA;
31cl Shutterstock/Vasily Smimov; 31bl SPL/Ria Novosti.

Contents

More to explore

On some of the pages in this book, you will find coloured buttons with symbols on them. There are four different colours, and each belongs to a different topic. Choose a topic, follow its coloured buttons through the book, and you'll make some interesting discoveries of your own.

For example, on page 7 you'll find a blue button, like this, near the people looking at the sky. The blue buttons are about people discovering space.

Page 19

Human exploration

There is a page number in the button. Turn to that page (page 19) to find a blue button next to another example of human exploration. Follow the steps through the book, and at the end of your journey you'll discover how the steps are linked and even more information about this topic.

Technology

Discovery

Science

The other topics in this book are technology, discovery and science. Follow the steps and see what you can discover!

All about space

Earth is our home in space. The Sun, the Moon, the stars and everything else beyond Earth are all in space. All these things together make the Universe. The Universe was born more than 13 billion years ago.

Mars

Mars's surface is covered in red soil.

Jupiter

Eight planets are in the part of space close to the Sun. Four of them are smaller planets made of rock and metal. They include Earth and Mars. Jupiter is one of the other four planets, which are much bigger and made mostly of gas.

Stars are huge spinning balls of hot, glowing gas. There are billions of them in space. The closest star to Earth is the Sun. The rest are so far away that they look like pinpoints of sparkling light.

From space, you can see Earth's land, oceans and clouds.

Some planets have moons. This is one of Mars's two moons.

Earth's surface is about one quarter land and the rest is water. Earth is the only place in space where we know there is life.

The Sun gives Earth light and warmth.

What is this?

① Planet Jupiter is brighter than the stars.

② Earth's Moon, lit up by the Sun

③ pinkish-red light from the setting Su[n]

Page 14

Night-time stars

Earth's sky is full of stars and other things in space. We can see them once the Sun has set and the sky has grown dark. Some stars are brighter than others. Venus, Jupiter and other distant planets can look like bright stars, too.

6

5

Page 19

Campers gaze up at the sky on a cloudless night. They can see the Moon, two planets and countless stars. All of the stars that are visible at night – and our daytime Sun, too – belong to a huge collection of stars known as a galaxy. Our galaxy is called the Milky Way because its stars make a milky path of light across the sky.

This is a meteor – a streak of light made by space dust shooting through Earth's atmosphere.

Brilliant stars

Stars in the night sky might look the same but each one is unique. Stars are different sizes, colours and temperatures, and some shine more brightly than others. Stars don't last forever. They are born, change as they age, and eventually die.

Sirius

This white dwarf star lives with Sirius in space.

Sirius is the brightest star in the night sky. This huge white star is twice as big as the Sun and 25 times brighter.

The Cat's Eye Nebula is a star near the end of its life. It has pushed off its outer layers of gas and these have made colourful, cloudy shells. They surround what's left of the central star.

Cat's Eye Nebula, a dying star

Constellations are imaginary patterns in the night sky made by joining up the brightest stars. This constellation is called the Swan.

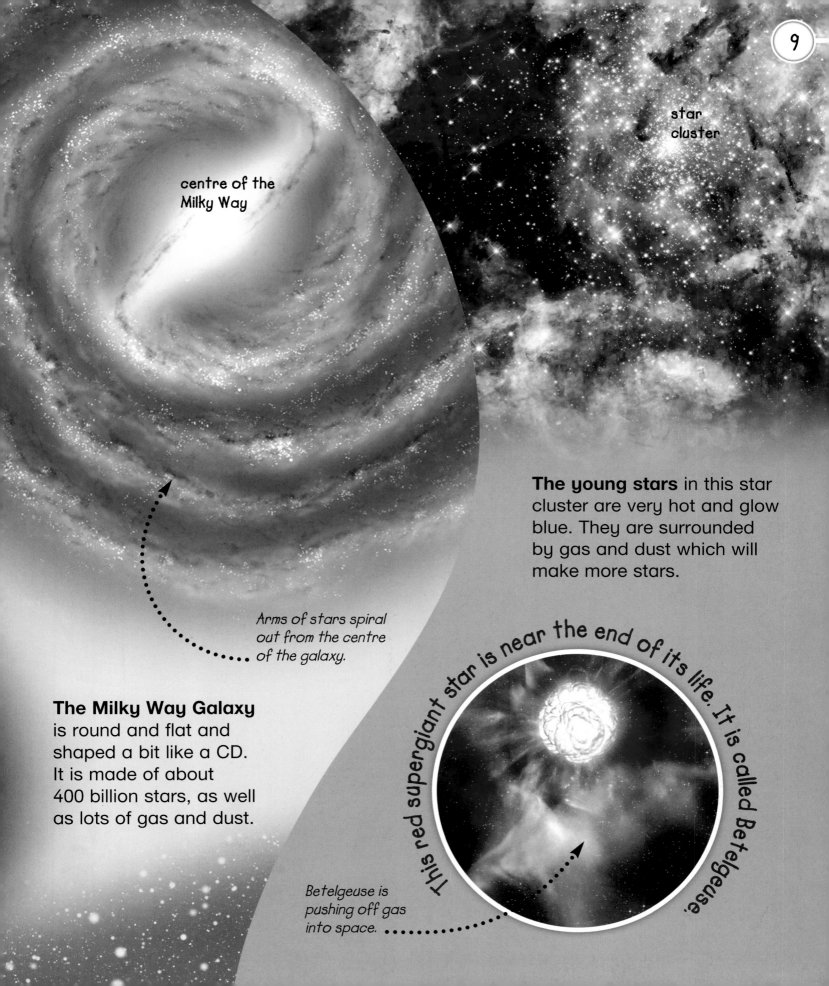

star cluster

centre of the Milky Way

The young stars in this star cluster are very hot and glow blue. They are surrounded by gas and dust which will make more stars.

Arms of stars spiral out from the centre of the galaxy.

The Milky Way Galaxy is round and flat and shaped a bit like a CD. It is made of about 400 billion stars, as well as lots of gas and dust.

This red supergiant star is near the end of its life. It is called Betelgeuse.

Betelgeuse is pushing off gas into space.

Space neighbour

The closest object to Earth in space is the Moon. It is a huge ball of rock that travels round our planet. It appears as the biggest, brightest thing in our night sky. The Moon doesn't have any light of its own, though – it shines brightly because sunlight bounces off its surface.

What is this?

Page 27

1. model of a spacecraft that landed on the Moon
2. photo of the Moon partly lit by sunshine
3. binoculars for viewing the Moon

? This is a map of the Moon's surface. It shows the sites of different Moon landings.

Page 30

Page 26

6

A young girl gazes out of her window at the Moon. Tonight it is full, which means she can see the whole disc. She has just recorded its shape in her notebook. She can see the Moon's highlands and lowlands as brighter and darker areas. Binoculars or a telescope provide a close-up view of the Moon's dry surface, which is covered in craters.

4 drawings of the Moon made at different dates

5 poster showing the Moon's path around Earth

6 A telescope shows the Moon in close-up.

On the Moon

The Moon has been studied a lot because it is so close to Earth. Thanks to telescopes and robot explorers we have photos and maps of its whole surface. Astronauts have also visited the Moon and brought back some of its rock.

Inside this spacesuit is Buzz Aldrin, the second person to walk on the Moon.

viewing the Moon

An astronaut is someone who travels into space. Twenty-four astronauts have flown as far as the Moon and 12 of them landed on its surface.

A telescope shows mountains, flat plains and thousands of small craters on the surface of the Moon.

Astronauts left footprints in the Moon's fine-grained soil

Buzz Aldrin's footprint

new Moon – its
face is unlit

waxing
crescent

first
quarter

waxing
gibbous

full Moon – its
face is fully lit

waning
gibbous

last
quarter

waning
crescent

A lunar rover is an electric car
built for driving across the Moon.
Three spacecraft took rovers and
astronauts to the Moon. The men
returned to Earth but the three
rovers are still there.

*The rover carried
astronauts and
the Moon rocks
they collected.*

There are round craters all over the Moon's surface.

*Space rocks made
craters when they
crashed into the
Moon billions of
years ago.*

The Moon
takes about a
month to travel
around the Earth.
As it moves,
different parts of
it are lit by the Sun.
This makes it look
as if the Moon is
changing shape. The
different shapes are
called phases. Some
have special names.

Page 27

What is this?

1	Sun	2	Mercury	3	Venus
7	Jupiter	8	Saturn	9	Uranus

11

9

12

5

7

Nearby space

Our Earth and Moon are part of the Solar System –
a family of space objects that travel around the Sun.
The Sun is the biggest object in the Solar System. Next
in size are the eight planets. There are also billions of small
bodies such as dwarf planets, moons, asteroids and comets

Page 30

This is what we would see if we could travel away from Earth and beyond the Solar System planets. It also shows the planets' paths, or orbits, around the Sun. The rock and metal planets – Mercury, Venus, Earth and Mars – are closest to the Sun. Further out is the largest planet, Jupiter, then Saturn, Uranus and Neptune. These four all have rings. Far beyond, in distant space, are the stars of the Milky Way.

This is an asteroid: a lump of rock in the Asteroid Belt between Mars and Jupiter.

Different worlds

When we look closely at the Solar System objects we can see they are very different worlds. They differ in size, what they are made of, and what their surfaces are like. The objects closest to the Sun are hottest. Things get colder and darker the further you travel from the Sun.

Callisto

Ganymede

Europa

Io

Jupiter has the most moons – more than 60! The largest four are Ganymede, Callisto, Io and Europa. Ganymede is the biggest moon in the Solar System.

The Sun is made of hot gas all the way through and does not have a solid surface. Jets of gas are bursting out of it all the time.

jets of gas bigger than Earth

When Comet Hale-Bopp moved close to the Sun it grew two tails.

white dust tail
and blue gas tail

Saturn

There are billions of asteroids in the Asteroid Belt.

·········· This asteroid is called Gaspra.

The picture below shows the **dwarf planet Pluto** in the sky of one of its moons, Charon. The two are both icy worlds about 40 times further from the Sun than the Earth.

icy, rocky Pluto

Saturn is a pale yellow colour but looks different here. The camera that took this picture used a type of light called ultraviolet light. It makes the different gases in Saturn's surface appear as different coloured bands.

Uranus has rings which seem to go around it from top to bottom. They are really around the planet's middle but Uranus is not upright. It was knocked over billions of years ago.

Uranus

Going into space

Anything going into space is taken there by a rocket. The journey starts on a launch pad where the rocket waits to lift off the ground. On board is its cargo – a spacecraft heading for a planet, or a craft with astronauts inside.

Two astronauts and their spacecraft are in the nose-end of a rocket waiting to blast off. The rocket's supporting framework is lowering away. Another rocket is just lifting off. Once in the air its first part, or stage, falls away. Its second stage continues into space where it releases the spacecraft to travel onwards on its own.

Page 15

What is this?

1 robotic spacecraft inside rocket

2 First stage lifts the rocket off the ground.

3 Control Centre where c team manages the launch

? This is a radio dish. It picks up radio signals from spacecraft in space, so they can be tracked.

4

Page 23

Page 23

5

6

4 astronauts inside
their spacecraft

5 rocket on launch pad

6 fuel inside the rocket

Space journey

A rocket's job is to get a spacecraft into space. It takes months to build, but its work is done in a few minutes. The spacecraft's mission can last days or years. Robotic spacecraft, which have no astronauts on board, can stay in space forever.

A rocket is used just once. A new one is built for each space journey. When it is ready, it is moved to its launch pad where its tanks are filled with fuel.

Soyuz rocket

Flight controllers are people who watch over a spacecraft once it has been launched. They follow its journey day and night until the craft finishes its mission.

The Soyuz rocket is put together lying down and then raised upright for its launch.

Soyuz-FG

Hot gas comes
out of the rocket's
first stage and four
booster rockets.

Green dye released
into the sea makes
the spacecraft
easy to spot.

**Astronauts returning
to Earth** usually land in
their home country but
these two came down in
the ocean. A waiting ship took
them back to the shore.

Ariane 5

booster
rocket

The first person in space was Yuri Gagarin in 1961.

Gagarin was
in space for 108 minutes.

Rockets come
in different sizes
depending on their
cargo. The Ariane 5 is
one of the biggest – as
tall as a 15-storey building.
It can carry three spacecraft
at once. The Soyuz-FG carries
people and is smaller and slimmer.

Spacewalk

Astronauts go outside their spacecraft for all sorts of reasons – to build space stations, repair broken spacecraft or to carry out experiments. During a spacewalk, astronauts wear spacesuits to protect them and supply them with oxygen gas to breathe.

Two astronauts are spacewalking outside the International Space Station – a huge spacecraft travelling round Earth 15 times a day. They have been fixing a new part to the station. Their tools are specially designed for their gloved hands. They are attached to tool belts so that they don't float off into space.

Page 30

What is this?

(1) Earth below has blue oceans and white clouds.

(2) Parts of the station are called modules.

(3) Spacesuit protects the astronaut's body

? This is an astronaut's glove. Heaters in the fingertips keep the astronaut's hand warm.

Page 11

Page 30

4 Hand drill is powered by batteries.

5 Helmet contains a phone system so the astronauts can talk to each other.

6 A checklist worn on the sleeve lists the jobs to do.

Living in space

Astronauts are living in space right now on the International Space Station. They work, relax and eat just as we do on Earth. But one big difference is that astronauts feel weightless and float about.

Sleeping bags are fixed to the space station's walls so sleeping astronauts don't move about. The astronauts have eight hours of rest and are woken by a different piece of music each day.

The astronaut's arms are weightless and move about as he sleeps.

astronaut on treadmill

Harness stops the astronaut floating away.

Astronauts exercise for at least two hours each day. Their bodies don't have to work so hard in weightless space, so the muscles weaken if they don't get plenty of exercise.

EVA or extra-vehicular activity is the correct name for a spacewalk. Only those astronauts going on EVA wear spacesuits.

new part to fix to space station

The International Space Station is a space home and workplace. It was launched in parts and then fitted together by spacewalking astronauts. It is about the size of a football pitch.

Solar panels make electricity for the space station.

space food

Some space foods are ready to eat; others need water adding or heating. Astronauts eat three meals a day as well as snacks and drinks.

This astronaut is ready to go on EVA.

Under the spacesuit, the astronaut wears a special undergarment. It contains tubes of water to keep his body cool.

Fresh fruit is brought by astronauts arriving at the station.

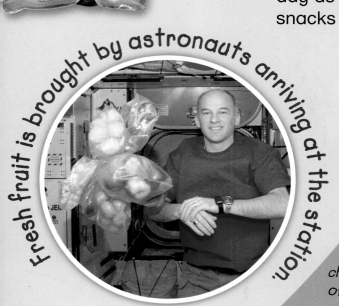

Tubes contain cooled water.

checklist of EVA work

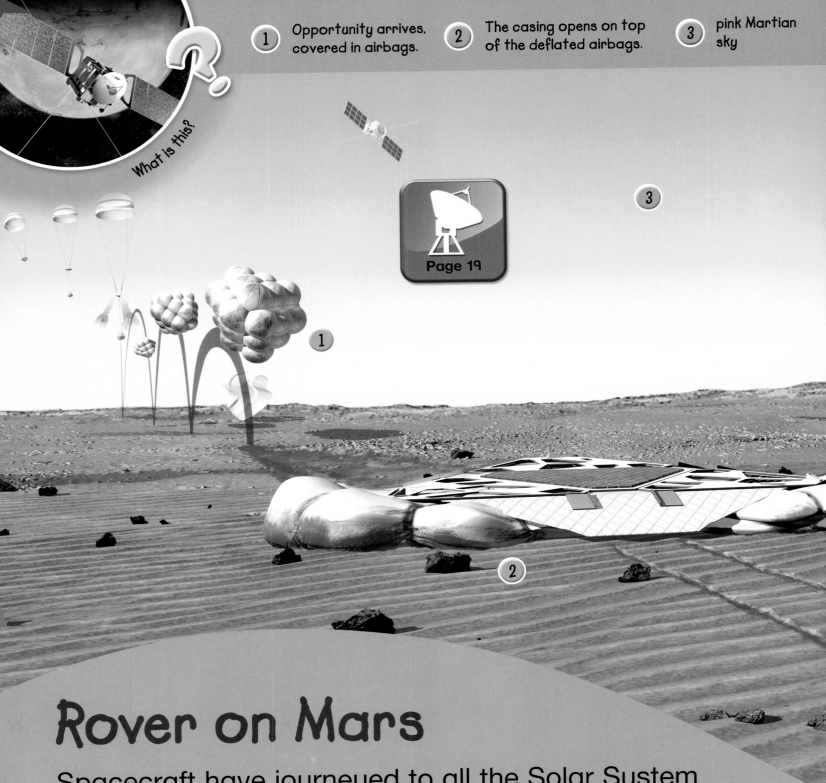

What is this?

1 Opportunity arrives. covered in airbags.

2 The casing opens on top of the deflated airbags.

3 pink Martian sky

Page 19

Rover on Mars

Spacecraft have journeyed to all the Solar System planets. The craft look down and take photographs as they fly past these distant worlds, or as they journey around them. Some land and investigate. A few of these, called rovers, drive across their surfaces.

Opportunity has been exploring Mars ever since it arrived in 2004. Inflated airbags protected the rover as it landed. After bouncing and rolling, it stopped and the airbags deflated. Then its casing opened and the rover drove off. Opportunity moves slowly across Mars. Every few metres it stops to study its surroundings.

Page 22

Page 18

This is Mars Express, a spacecraft that takes photos of Mars as it travels around it.

Robot explorers

Some spacecraft explore distant worlds that are too dangerous or too far away for astronauts to visit. Onboard computers tell these robot explorers what to do. The craft also receive extra instructions sent by radio from Earth.

Signals from the dish take 90 minutes to reach Earth.

Cassini is travelling around Saturn and some of its moons. It gave a ride to a smaller craft called Huygens, which it released to parachute down to the surface of Saturn's largest moon, Titan.

Voyager 1 is the furthest spacecraft from Earth. It was launched in 1977 and flew past Jupiter in 1979, and Saturn in 1980. Now it is heading out of the Solar System.

Cameras are the robot's eyes.

photo of Beagle Crater on Mars by Opportunity

Opportunity

Opportunity and its twin, Spirit (also on Mars), have taken pictures of the planet's surface. They show us what we would see if we could walk on Mars.

Cassini

Rosetta is on its way to a comet. It will arrive in 2014 after a 10-year trip from Earth. Then it will journey with the comet as it travels round the Sun.

Rosetta passed by the asteroid Steins as it journeyed through the Asteroid Belt.

Jupiter

Jupiter's moon, Io

New Horizons has flown by Jupiter and is on target to arrive at the dwarf planet Pluto in 2015. As it flies by, its seven instruments will find out what Pluto is made of, how cold it is, and map its surface.

electric generator provides power

photo of Africa by Landsat

Satellites are spacecraft that travel round Earth. Some photograph our planet from space. They study its land, oceans, ice and atmosphere. The Landsat satellites have been watching over Earth for 40 years.

Landsat

Discovery

Looking into the night sky is a great way to discover things in space. You may be lucky enough to spot a **meteor** (shooting star) – or even a whole shower of them.

Comets are huge, dirty snowballs that exist far out in space, beyond the planets. Occasionally a comet travels near to our Sun. Then it is big enough and bright enough to be seen in Earth's sky.

Science

notebook

By recording **observations**, scientists notice patterns and can predict events. That is how people discovered the lunar phases are repeated every 29.5 days. Lunar means 'to do with the Moon'.

Solar means 'to do with the Sun'. The **solar panels** on the Martian rover turn sunlight into electricity. This is stored in batteries and used to power the craft and its equipment.

Human exploration

telescopes, Hawaii

People who study the stars and planets are called **astronomers**. The first used just their eyes to view the night sky. Today, telescopes and spacecraft help astronomers see more than ever.

Just over 500 **astronauts** have been into space. They are mostly men but include more than 50 women. They have come from about 40 different nations.

rocket carrying crew to the ISS

Technology

A telescope collects light from an object in space and uses it to produce a magnified image. This helpful tool lets us see things more clearly and in greater detail.

Orbiters such as Mars Express are spacecraft that travel around planets or other objects in the Solar System. Orbiters work for a few years, mapping the whole surface of the planet and testing its atmosphere.

Mars Express

More to explore

Cameras on spacecraft show us things we cannot see from Earth. Images are recorded on the craft's computer and then sent to Earth as radio signals.

cameras on Opportunity rover

Onboard the **International Space Station** (ISS), astronauts are finding out what it is like to live in space for months at a time. Their experience will help plan for a future trip to the planet Mars.

ISS

A rocket is powered by engines that burn fuel and produce hot gas. This gas pushes out of the bottom end of the rocket at high speed. The rocket is forced upwards in the opposite direction to the gas.

A force called gravity keeps all the planets on their paths, or **orbits**, around the Sun. The Earth takes a year to make one complete path.

Spacewalks usually last several hours and the astronauts are kept busy the whole time. Astronauts have spent a total of about 800 hours spacewalking outside the ISS.

spacewalking astronaut

The Moon is the only world apart from Earth that humans have visited. Twelve men have walked on its surface. The first manned mission to land was in 1969, and the last was in 1972.

the Moon

Rockets have been going into space for 60 years. They lift off from about 30 launch sites around the world. Only three countries have built rockets to launch astronauts – the USA, Russia and China.

Spacesuits give astronauts their own Earth-like environment. They are made of many layers of material which hold in the oxygen and keep astronauts at a constant temperature.

Index